Detective.

Volume 2

A Quiz Game for Kids & All the Family

By
Mark Lloyd

Published by
Pillar International Publishing Ltd
www.IndiePillar.com

© Mark Lloyd 2017
All Rights Reserved

Book and Cover Design by Lotte Bender
Cover Illustration by Lotte Bender

ISBN: 978-1-911303-10-7

Dedication

To everyone who bought and loved Detective!
Volume 1

Introduction

The *Detective!* games came about almost by accident. It formed a small part of another quiz book - "The Clever Kid's Quiz and Puzzle Book" – but when I saw how much fun the kids had with it I decided to dedicate a whole book to the concept.

December 2016 saw me touring the country, attending Christmas Fairs, selling books. *Detective!* proved to be a huge favourite with the kids who called to the stall, so I decided to produce another two volumes, of which this is the first. If you haven't already bought them, you should keep an eye out for the other volumes.

Enjoy!

Mark.

Direct any feedback or corrections to:
info@indiepillar.com.

Detective!

Detective is a guessing game. You need at least two people to play. First, one person is the quizmaster and they must ask all of the questions. The others can be the contestants.

The idea is that the quizmaster reads out clues and the participant(s) must try to guess the answer using the clues. Points are awarded depending on how many clues the participant needs to solve the riddle.

Get it right on 1st clue   = 10 points
Get it right on 2nd clue   = 8 points
Get it right on 3rd clue   = 6 points
Get it right on 4th clue   = 4 points
Get it right on 5th clue   = 2 points

So, appoint a quizmaster. Read each clue one at a time and allow the participant twenty seconds to come up with a single guess after each clue has been read. Don't expect to get too many correct guesses after the first clue – although you could be lucky!

This is great fun at parties, in classrooms and on car journeys and, once you know how to play, you can have a go making up your own questions.

(Answers at the back of the book!)

Game 1:
Case File 1

I am in Europe

I am in France

I am a city

Pronounced differently, I can mean 'to be pleasant or well-behaved'

I begin with the letter 'N'

Game 1:
Case File 2

I am a fruit

I am native to Mexico

My skin is green and uneven

My yellow/green flesh is used in Guacamole

I am pear-shaped and begin with 'Avo'

Game 1:
Case File 3

I am a musical instrument

I can be large

I have strings

I am often associated with Ireland

I begin with the letter 'H'

Game 1:
Case File 4

I am a game

I am very popular on TV.

I am also popular in bars

I contain questions

I begin with the letter 'Q'

Game 1:
Case File 5

I am something you eat

I am also used to make drinks

I can be white, milk or dark

You might have me for dessert

I am a flavour of Ice-Cream

Game 1:
Case File 6

I am a country in Europe

My flag is yellow and blue

My capital city is Stockholm

I am associated with Zlatan Ibrahimovic

I begin with an 'S'

Game 1:
Case File 7

I am an invention

I involve hooks and loops

I am used in footwear and jackets

I make a ripping sound when I am opened

I begin with a 'V'

Game 1:
Case File 8

I am a something you wear

I can be camp, dress, Henley or polo

In French I am called a chemise

Normally, I have cuffs and a collar

I begin with the letter 'S'

Game 1:
Case File 9

I am a country

I am a *large* country

My national languages are English and French

I am in North America

I am above the USA

Game 1:
Case File 10

I am part of your body

I am beneath your waist

I am where the tibia, fibula and talus meet

I am where the foot and the leg meet

I am a joint beginning with 'A'

Game 2:
Case File 1

I am something written

I am normally on paper but can be online

Samuel Pepys wrote a famous version of me

I am usually written every day

I begin with the letter 'D'

Game 2:
Case File 2

I am a country in Europe

I was the birthplace of Marie Antoinette

Before the Euro my currency was the schilling

My capital city is Vienna

I begin with the letter 'A'

Game 2:
Case File 3

I am an article of clothing

I am sometimes made of leather

I have a buckle

I stop your trousers falling down

I begin with the letter 'B'

Game 2:
Case File 4

I am an invention

I can be made from processed animal parts

Another word for me is 'adhesive'

I help two things to stick together

I begin with the letter 'G'

Game 2:
Case File 5

I am a type of animal

I am also the name given to the language of Thailand

I am also a name given to conjoined-twins

I am a type of cat

I begin with the letter 'S'

Game 2:
Case File 6

I am a city

I am in Eastern Europe

I am home to St. Basil's Cathedral

I am home to Red Square

My inhabitants are called Muscovites

Game 2:
Case File 7

I am a place

You can work here

I can be 'Post', 'Home' or 'Back'

I normally have a door and a desk

I begin with the letter 'O'

Game 2:
Case File 8

I am a place

You can work here

There are food and other items here

You can buy things here in my large aisles

I begin with the letter 'S'

Game 2:
Case File 9

I am a colour

I am not one of the colours of the rainbow

You get me by mixing blue and red

I am the colour of Barney the Dinosaur

I begin with the letter 'P'

Game 2:
Case File 10

I am a fictional character

I have appeared in many films and comics

I am one of the X-Men

My real name is sometimes Logan

I begin with the letter 'W'

Game 3:
Case File 1

I am a type of animal

I am from the corvid family

I can be 'Pied', 'Hooded' or 'American'

I am a bird

I begin with the letter 'C'

Game 3:
Case File 2

I am a type of animal

I am from the rodent family

I can be 'European', 'Angora' or 'Golden'

I can be a pet

I begin with the letter 'H'

Game 3:
Case File 3

I am a type of animal

I can be found in the sea

I am a predator

I can be 'Tiger', 'Blue' or 'Hammerhead'

I being with the letter 'S'

Game 3:
Case File 4

I am something you own

I help to mind your money

You can take from me or put into me

I can be 'Current', 'Deposit' or 'Loan'

I am found in a bank

Game 3:
Case File 5

I am something you can eat

I am grown in the ground

I am a type of squash

I can be used to make lanterns (at Halloween)

I begin with the letter 'P'

Game 3:
Case File 6

I am a number

I am the number of innings in a baseball game

I am IX in Roman Numerals

I am *nueve* in Spanish

I begin with 'N'

Game 3:
Case File 7

I am a job or a type of movie

I work with animals

I am associated with the 'Wild-West'

I work on horse-back

I begin with the letter 'C'

Game 3:
Case File 8

I am a type of plant

I am a vegetable

I am normally tall and light green

My stalks are great for dips

I begin with the letter 'C'

Game 3:
Case File 9

I am a type of building

I am made for people to gather

I can have an apse and a sacristy

I am associated with religion

I begin with a 'Ch' sound

Game 3:
Case File 10

I am a living thing

I have ten legs

I live in the sea

I am popular in curries

I can also be called 'Shrimp' and begin with the letter 'P'

Game 4:
Case File 1

I am something you might find in the kitchen

I am used in baking

I am associated normally with flour

I am full of holes

I begin with the letter 'S'

Game 4:
Case File 2

I am a person's name

I am a boy's name

I am the name of an English prince

I am the name of the patron Saint of Scotland

I begin with the letter 'A'

Game 4:
Case File 3

I am a person's name

I am a boy's name

I am associated with the Bible

I helped free the slaves from Egypt

I begin with the letter 'M'

Game 4:
Case File 4

I am something you can eat

I can be found in sandwiches

I am associated with a famous gorge

I am a type of cheese

I begin with the letter 'C'

Game 4:
Case File 5

I am something you can do

It is said that I originated in India

I involve 'poses'

I can be used for exercise and meditation

I begin with the letter 'Y'

Game 4:
Case File 6

I am a place

I am a sporting venue

I am the home of The Surrey County Cricket Club

I am also the name of a shape

I begin with the letter 'O'

Game 4:
Case File 7

I am a material

I can come in reams

My name comes from the Latin word 'Papyrus'

I am normally made from pulped trees

You can write or draw on me

Game 4:
Case File 8

I am a planet

I was once called Le Verrier's planet

I am also a Roman god

I am the 8th planet in our Solar System

I begin with the letter 'N'

Game 4:
Case File 9

I am a famous person

I am an author

I was born in Wales in 1915 to Norwegian parents

I am famous for writing children's books

I wrote 'The BFG'

Game 4:
Case File 10

I am something you can hold in your hand

I am normally made of metal

I can be found in a toolbox

I am used to loosen things

I begin with the letter 'S'

Game 5:
Case File 1

I am a thing sometimes made of found objects

I am associated with animals

I can also be used to describe tables

I can be found in trees

I am the name for a bird's home

Game 5:
Case File 2

I am a living thing

You can eat me

I am eaten raw or cooked

I live in the sea

I begin with the letter 'O'

Game 5:
Case File 3

I am a TV Show

By 2016, I have been made in 11 different countries

My title is eight words long

I was first won in 2002 by Tony Blackburn

My initials are IAC…
GMOOH

Game 5:
Case File 4

I am a place

I am tourist attraction

I am in London

I am associated with the Crown Jewels

I am a tower that was once a prison

Game 5:
Case File 5

I am a living thing

I am native to Borneo and Sumatra

I am an endangered species

I am a type of ape

I begin with the letter 'O'

Game 5:
Case File 6

I am something you might find in your kitchen

I am normally in liquid form

I am used for cleaning

You can squirt me

I can be used to make bubbles

Game 5:
Case File 7

I am a character from books and films

I can normally be seen wearing a red shirt

I was created by A.A. Milne

I like honey

I have a friend called Tigger

Game 5:
Case File 8

I am a series of books and films

The main character is called Greg

I was created by Jeff Kinney

Greg has a brother called Roderick

My initials are DOAWK

Game 5:
Case File 9

I am something you can eat

I am sweet-tasting

I am made of water, sugar and gelatin

I am normally the shape of a small cylinder

I am great on hot-chocolate or s'mores

Game 5:
Case File 10

I am a herb

I am also a type of sweet

I am great with lamb

I am also a flavour of ice-cream

I begin with the letter 'M'

Game 6:
Case File 1

I am a toy

I am played with by small children

I can feature a winder and a spring

My name includes a boy's name

My initials are JITB

Game 6:
Case File 2

I am a material used to make things

There are many types of me

I can be bendy or stretchy

I can melt when too hot

I am used to make bin bags, for example

Game 6:
Case File 3

I am a tourist attraction

I am in France

I am in Paris

I am an Art Gallery

I begin with the letter 'L'

Game 6:
Case File 4

I am a type of person

I feature in many books and films

I am not honest

I normally sail in a ship

I sometimes have a parrot and a wooden leg

Game 6:
Case File 5

I am a living thing

I am a fish

I can be found in an aquarium

I am named for my colour

I begin with the letter 'G'

Game 6:
Case File 6

I am something you might find on a map of England

Part of me also known as the Isis

I am a river

I flow through London

I am the longest river in England

Game 6:
Case File 7

I am a name for a leader

I am used in the army

I am also used in soccer and rugby

I am also used on a ship

I begin with the letter 'C'

Game 6:
Case File 8

I am a cartoon character

I was created by Hanna-Barbera in 1958

I am an animal

I love picnic baskets

I have a small friend called Boo-boo

Game 6:
Case File 9

I am part of your body

I am below your waist

There are ten of me

I can be painted

I begin with the letter 'T'

Game 6:
Case File 10

I am a toy

I have been around for over 2000 years

I involve disks and string or cord

I go up and down

I begin with the letter 'Y'

Game 7:
Case File 1

I am a something you might find on a map of America

I am a river

I am also the name of a U.S. State

My name contains four 'i's

I begin with the letter 'M'

Game 7:
Case File 2

I am a sports venue

I am in England

I am in London

I am associated with Tennis

I begin with the letter 'W'

Game 7:
Case File 3

I am a place

I am in America

My capital city is Sacramento

I am on the west coast

I begin with the letter 'C'

Game 7:
Case File 4

I am a tourist attraction

I was built in 1999

I am in England

I am in London

I am a big Ferris wheel

Game 7:
Case File 5

I am something you might find in your house

I sometimes need water

I help keep clothes looking smart

I am also the name of a metal

I am also the name of a golf club

Game 7:
Case File 6

I was invented by Alexander Godefroy

I need to be plugged in

I am used for getting rid of water

I can be found in salons and can be hand-held or hood

I am used on wet hair

Game 7:
Case File 7

I am a character from a movie

I am from Star Wars

I am a Jedi

I am old and small

I begin with the letter 'Y'

Game 7:
Case File 8

I am a material

China is the biggest producer of me

I grow on a plant

I am used to make clothes

I begin with the letter 'C'

Game 7:
Case File 9

I am a well-known woman

I was born in America in 1897

I disappeared on July 2nd 1937

I was a pilot

My initials are AE

Game 7:
Case File 10

I am an invention

My first version was released in 2007

My seventh version was unveiled in 2016

I have a touch screen

I am a type of phone made by Apple

Game 8:
Case File 1

I am an ingredient

I am thought to have come from Turkey

I am used in cakes and buns

I am a dried fruit

I am sometimes confused with a raisin

Game 8:
Case File 2

I am something you use

I can be manual or electric

I can be flat-headed or Phillips

You can find me in your toolbox

I begin with the letter 'S'

Game 8:
Case File 3

I am a type of fruit

I am found on a palm tree

I am mentioned more than 50 times in the bible

You might also find me on a calendar

I begin with the letter 'D'

Game 8:
Case File 4

I am a famous woman

I was an actress, director and writer

I was once married to Paul Simon

My mother was actress Debbie Reynolds

I played Princess Leia

Game 8:
Case File 5

I am something you eat

I am sweet

I am made with eggs

I am associated with trifle

I begin with the letter 'C'

Game 8:
Case File 6

I am a fruit

In French I am called *ananas*

There are two syllables in my name

I am sometimes put onto pizza

I begin with the letter 'P'

Game 8:
Case File 7

I am an invention

I was created by Tim Berners-Lee

I am connected to computers

My abbreviation has three letters

The first is 'W'

Game 8:
Case File 8

I am a something found in an office

I can also be in the house

You can connect to me via your computer

I can be colour or black and white

You put paper in me

Game 8:
Case File 9

I am something you eat

I can be salted or unsalted

I melt when hot

I am made from milk

You can put me on toast

Game 8:
Case File 10

I am an ingredient

I am made up of carbon, hydrogen and oxygen

On average, you consume 24kg of me a year

I am bad for your teeth!

I am used to make sweets

Game 9:
Case File 1

I am a type of fictional character

I have appeared in movies and books

I am associated with horror

I am neither alive nor dead

I begin with the letter 'Z'

Game 9:
Case File 2

I am something you can eat

I can be many flavours

I am a dessert

I am normally on a base of biscuits

I involve cheese

Game 9:
Case File 3

I am something you can eat

I am a vegetable

I am green and taste good with melted butter

I am long and thin, like fingers

I begin with the letter 'A'

Game 9:
Case File 4

I am part of your body

I am below the waist

I am a joint on your leg

I have a bone called a patella

I begin with the letter 'K'

Game 9:
Case File 5

I am a boy's name

I can also be something to do with a car

I am often used in nursery rhymes

I am associated with cards

I can sometimes be 'in-the-box'

Game 9:
Case File 6

I can be black or white

I am made from beans

I am also a shade of colour

I am something you can drink

I begin with the letter 'C'

Game 9:
Case File 7

I am a job title

I am associated with religion

I am in charge of a diocese

I am also a piece on a chessboard

I begin with the letter 'B'

Game 9:
Case File 8

I am a substance that is usually green

I am from a fictional story

I am named after my planet of origin

I weaken Superman

I begin with the letter 'K'

Game 9:
Case File 9

I am a sport

I take place on a field

I was first played in 1869

I am played by two teams of eleven players

I am associated with one country, and this country features in my name

Game 9:
Case File 10

I am company or corporation

I bought Instagram in 2012

I am associated with the internet

I was founded by Mark Zuckerberg

I begin with the letter 'F'

Game 10:
Case File 1

I am normally made of paper

I can have pictures on me

I can have monetary amounts on me

I can have glue on one side

I am stuck to an envelope

Game 10:
Case File 2

I am a living thing

I have four legs

I can be fast

I can be described as equine

You can sit on me

Game 10:
Case File 3

I am a girl's name

I am three letters long but I can also be four letters long

I was the name of two of Henry VIII's wives

I am associated with the names Hathaway and Bancroft

I begin with the letter 'A'

Game 10:
Case File 4

I am an adjective

I was also the name of a ship used by the US Navy in World War II

I can go before sand, lime and silver

I can mean speedy

I begin with the letter 'Q'

Game 10:
Case File 5

I am a country

I am in Africa

My official language is Arabic

My capital city is Cairo

I am associated with pyramids

Game 10:
Case File 6

I am a noun

I am associated with Rugby

I am associated with hair

I am associated with canals

You need a key to open me

Game 10:
Case File 7

I am a painting

My artist created four versions of me

I was stolen in 1994 and 2004

I am in the National Gallery in Oslo

I was painted by Edvard Munch in 1893

Game 10:
Case File 8

I am something you eat

There are two ways to pronounce me

I am a type of single-serving bread

I am associated with clotted cream

I begin with the letter 'S'

Game 10:
Case File 9

I am a city

I am in Europe

I was the site of Operation Vittles after World War II

I was the site of the 2006 Football World Cup final

I begin with the letter 'B'

Game 10:
Case File 10

I am a fictional character

I was first voiced by Clarence Nash

I was created in 1934

I am an male animal

I am a Disney Character beginning with the letter 'D'

ANSWERS!

Game 1

1.1. Nice

1.2. Avocado

1.3. Harp

1.4. Quiz

1.5. Chocolate

1.6. Sweden

1.7. Velcro

1.8. Shirt

1.9. Canada

1.10. Ankle

Game 2

2.1. Diary

2.2. Austria

2.3. Belt

2.4. Siamese

2.4. Glue

2.5. Moscow

2.6. Office

2.7. Supermarket

2.9. Purple

2.10. Wolverine

Game 3

3.1. Crow

3.2. Hamster

3.3. Shark

3.4. Bank Account

3.5. Pumpkin

3.6. Nine

3.7. Cowboy

3.8. Celery

3.9. Church

3.10. Prawns

Game 4

4.1. Sieve

4.2. Andrew

4.3. Moses

4.4. Cheddar

4.5. Yoga

4.6. The Oval

4.7. Paper

4.8. Neptune

4.9. Roald Dahl

4.10. Spanner

Game 5

5.1. Nest

5.2. Oyster

5.3. I'm a Celebrity, Get Me Out of Here

5.4. The Tower of London

5.5. Orangutan

5.6. Washing-up liquid

5.7. Winnie The Pooh

5.8. Diary of a Wimpy Kid

5.9. Marshmallow

5.10. Mint

Game 6

6.1. Jack-in-the-Box

6.2. Plastic

6.3. The Louvre

6.4. Pirate

6.5. Goldfish

6.6. The Thames

6.7. Captain

6.8. Yogi Bear

6.9. Toenail

6.10. Yo-yo

Game 7

7.1. The Mississippi

7.2. Wimbledon

7.3. California

7.4. The London Eye

7.5. Iron

7.6. Hair-dryer

7.7. Yoda

7.8. Cotton

7.9. Amelia Earhart

7.10. iPhone

Game 8

8.1. Sultana

8.2. Screwdriver

8.3. Date

8.4. Carrie Fisher

8.5. Custard

8.6. Pineapple

8.7. WWW

8.8. Printer

8.9. Butter

8.10. Sugar

Game 9

9.1. Zombie

9.2. Cheesecake

9.3. Asparagus

9.4. Knee

9.5. Jack

9.6. Coffee

9.7. Bishop

9.8. Kryptonite

9.9. American Football

9.10. Facebook

Game 10

10.1. Postage Stamp

10.2. Horse

10.3. Ann/Anne/Annie

10.4. Quick

10.5. Egypt

10.6. Lock

10.7. The Scream

10.8. Scone

10.9. Berlin

10.10. Donald Duck

Also Available from
Pillar International Publishing

The Clever Kid's Quiz and Puzzle Book
By Mark Lloyd

The Ready-Made Kids Quiz
by
Mark Lloyd

The Ready-Made Kids Quiz Vol. II
by
Mark Lloyd

The Weirdest Island Ever
by
Marvel Gumshoe

Books available on Amazon.com
and
in all decent bookshops